ARPEGGIOS AND PIECES IN ALL KEYS

BOOK ONE

JOHN W. SCHAUM, MUS. D.

Born in Milwaukee, Wisconsin. Founder and Director of the famous Schaum Piano School at Milwaukee. Mus. M., Northwestern University; Mus. B., Marquette University; B. Ed., Milwaukee Teachers' College; Unlimited state certificate to teach piano; 12 seasons on Shorewood Opportunity School Faculty; 9 years head of Piano Department at Milwaukee University School; soloist with Milwaukee Philharmonic Orchestra. Past President of Wisconsin Music Teachers' Association; Composer of many Original Compositions for the Piano. Editor and arranger of more than 300 Standard Pieces and Supplementary Books for the Young Piano Student. Composer of the famous "Schaum Note Speller" and the "Schaum Piano Course."

Printed in U. S. A.

Belwin Mills Publishing Corp.
MELVILLE, N.Y. 11746

CONTENTS

Ed. Libr. No. 219

YOUR ARPEGGIO RECORD

Teacher's Note: *Before the pupil studies this arpeggio book, he should review the exercises in Scales and Pieces in All Keys (Book 1) by John W. Schaum. Arpeggios are built on scales; therefore, the scale book is a prerequisite to arpeggio study.*

The key circle on this page is for you to record your arpeggio progress. As you learn each arpeggio with its accompanying piece, mark in the letters of the corresponding tonic chord. The key of C major is already marked as it should be. If done with red crayon your progress will show up clearly.

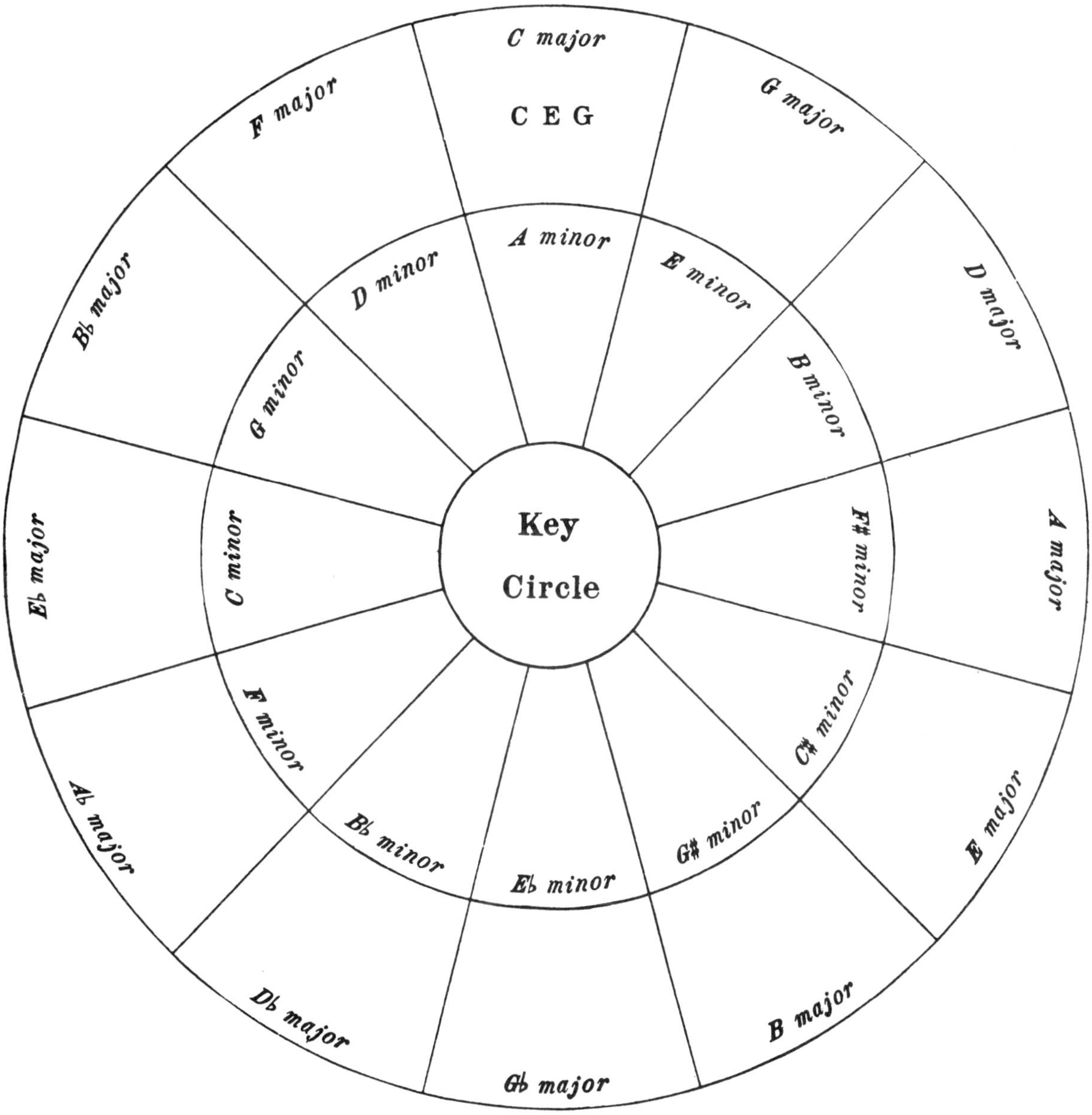

TONIC MAJOR ARPEGGIOS IN SHARPS

The word *arpeggio* is derived from the Italian word *arpa* (the harp.) Arpeggio, therefore, means to play *harp-like,* that is, to break or spread a chord either upward or downward. Arpeggios, which seldom have any *melodic* significance, are found chiefly in *accompaniments.*

Directions: Below, are the principal major sharp keys. The key of C major is marked as it should be. You are to write in the chords and arpeggios for the remaining keys.

C MAJOR ARPEGGIO

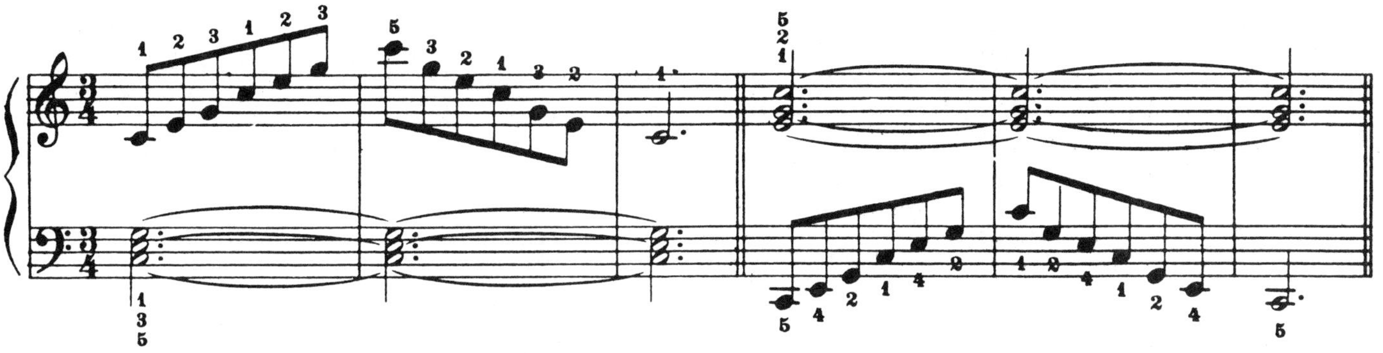

Also: F, G (Eb)

IVAN SKAVINSKY SKIVAR

Directions: Practice each piece in the book in two ways. First, do the arpeggios (indicated in brackets) in chord blocks. Second, play the piece as written. Draw a circle around all tonic arpeggios. Arpeggios other than tonic are used for variety. You will understand these when you study more about harmony. Don't worry about them now.

Teacher's Note: In Book II of *Arpeggios and Pieces in All Keys* by John W. Schaum, longer arpeggios will be used in the pieces. The arpeggios of the dominant seventh and the diminished seventh, also, will be presented.

hands sep first

G MAJOR ARPEGGIO

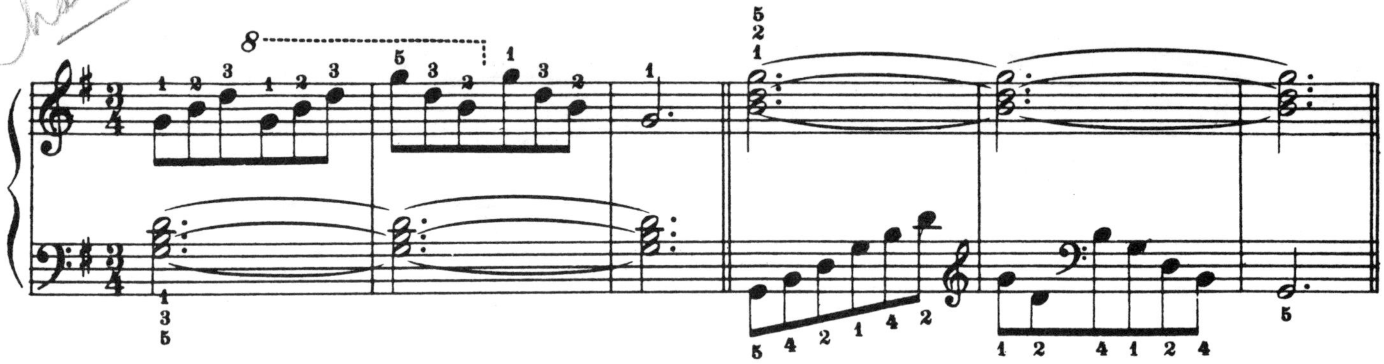

ALBERTI'S SONATA

Note the different manner of breaking the chord in the left hand. This type of arpeggio is known as the "Alberti Bass."

Domenico Alberti (1710 - 1740)
(Father of the Alberti Bass)

Allegretto

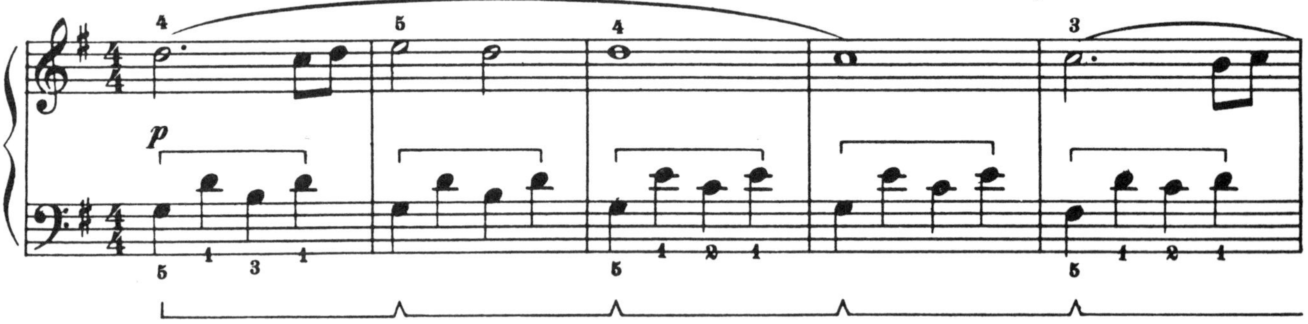

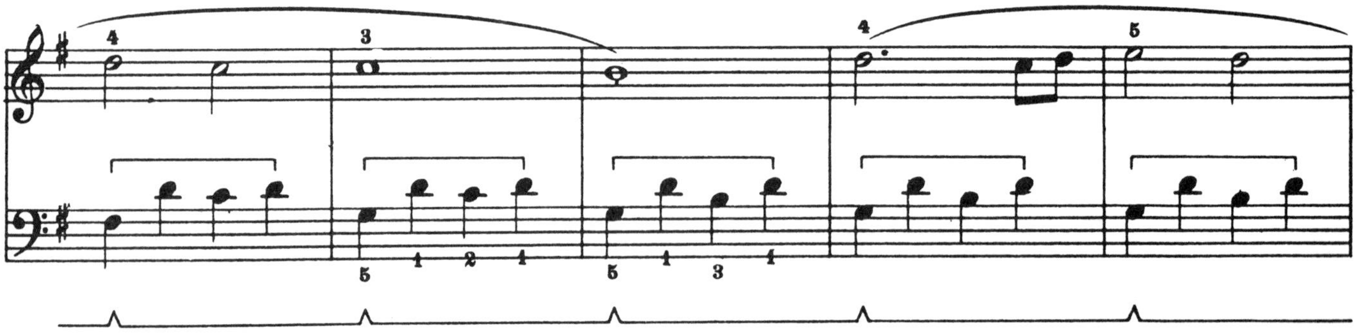

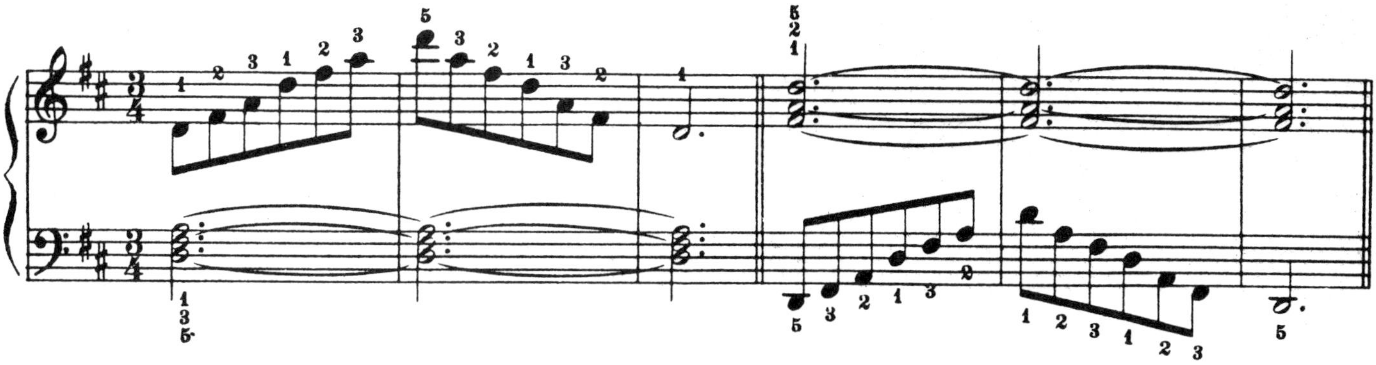

RONDO

Notice the Alberti Bass. Mozart used this very frequently.

Mozart
(1756-1791)

Allegretto

Only 2 bass chords

A MAJOR ARPEGGIO

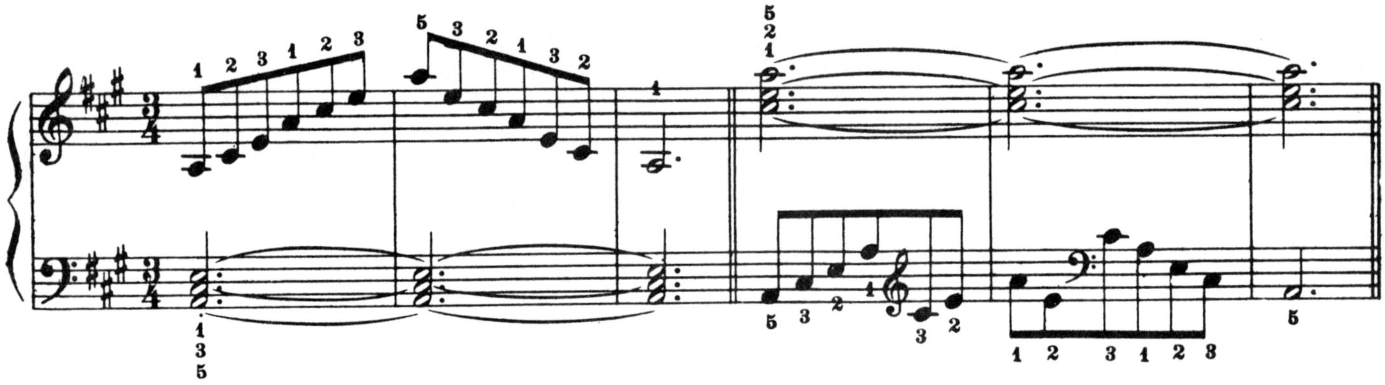

LA SPAGNOLA

Note: Most pieces begin and end on the tonic arpeggio or chord.

Tempo di Valse

V. di Chiara

E MAJOR ARPEGGIO

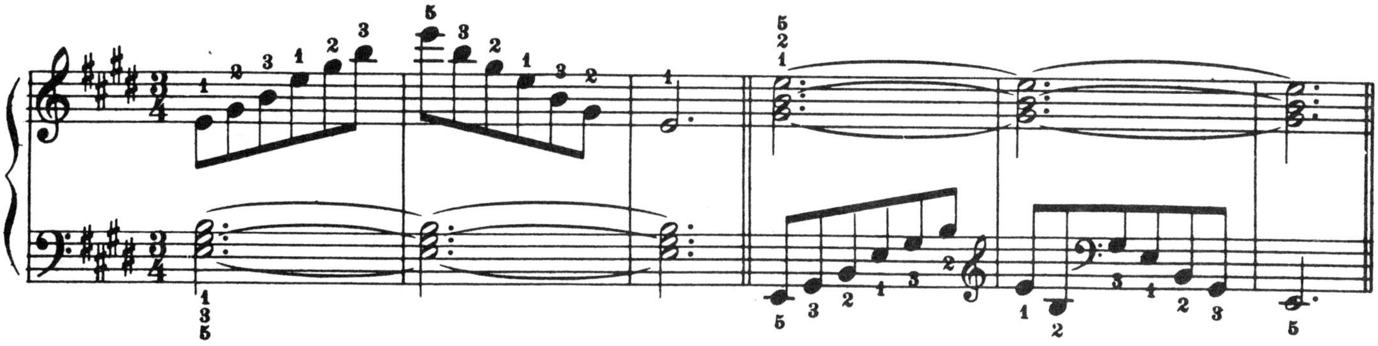

LOVE SONG

Note: Always draw circles around the tonic arpeggios in all pieces throughout the entire book.

A. Henselt

Andantino

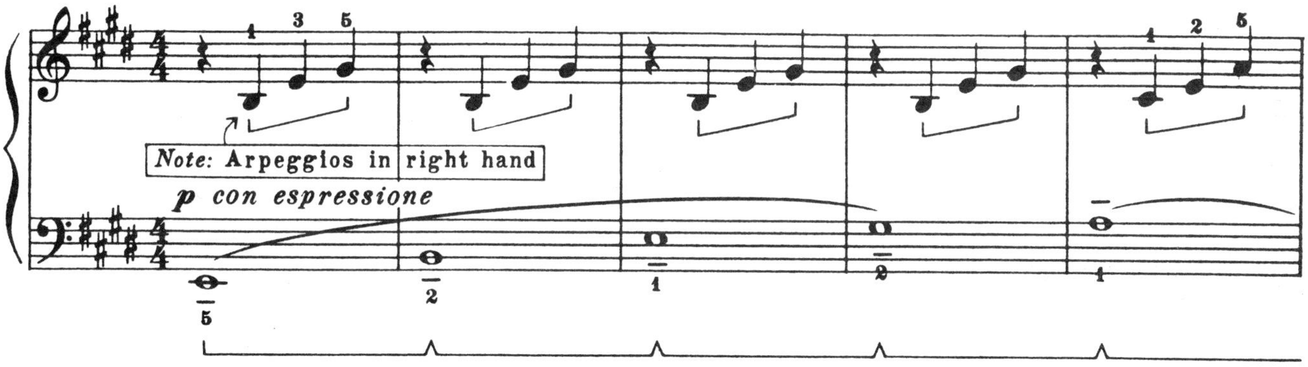

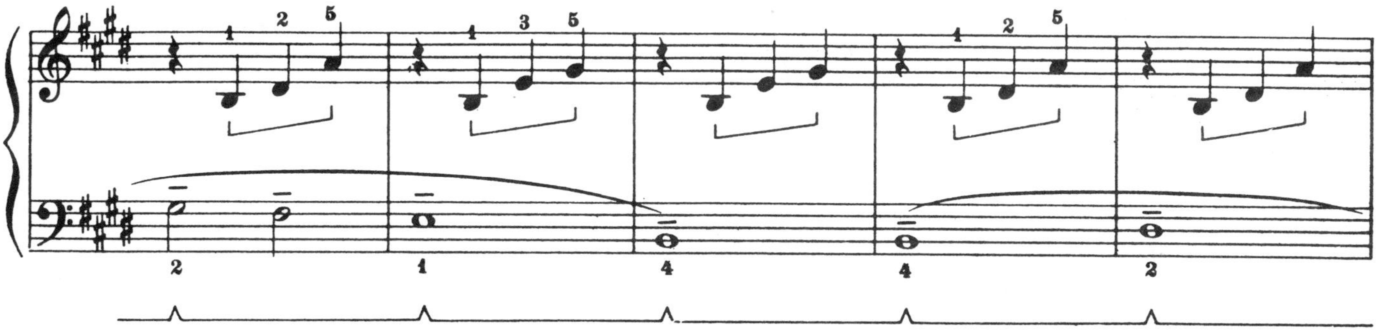

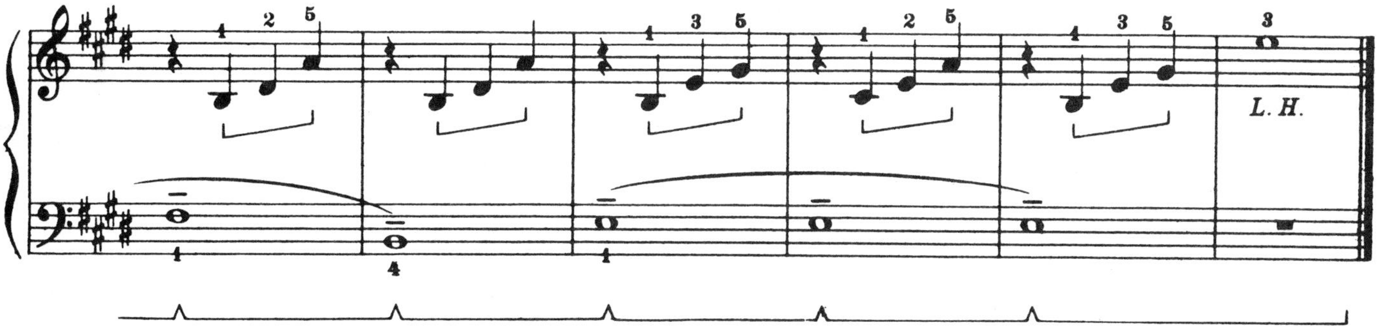

B MAJOR ARPEGGIO

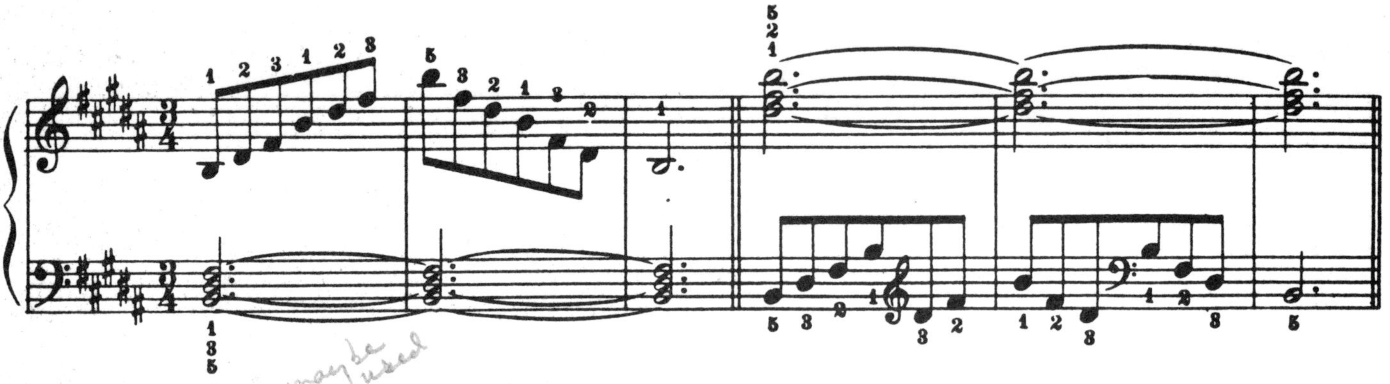

Note: B+E not sharped
All the black keys may be used

HEATHER ROSE

G. Lange

TONIC MAJOR ARPEGGIOS IN FLATS

Directions: Below are the principal major flat keys. You are to write in the three tonic chord positions and arpeggios for each key as you did on page four.

F major chord positions

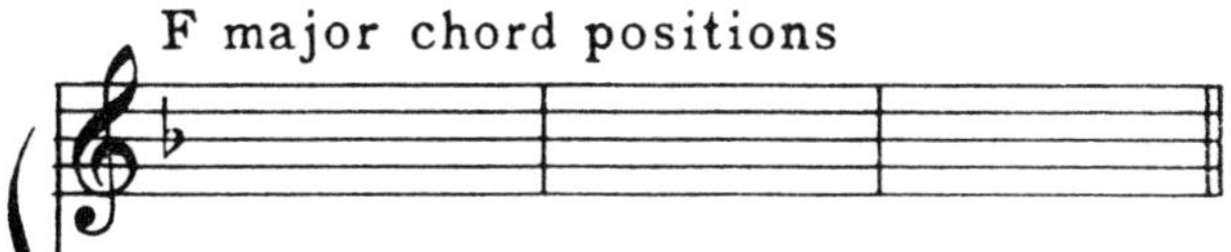

F major arpeggios

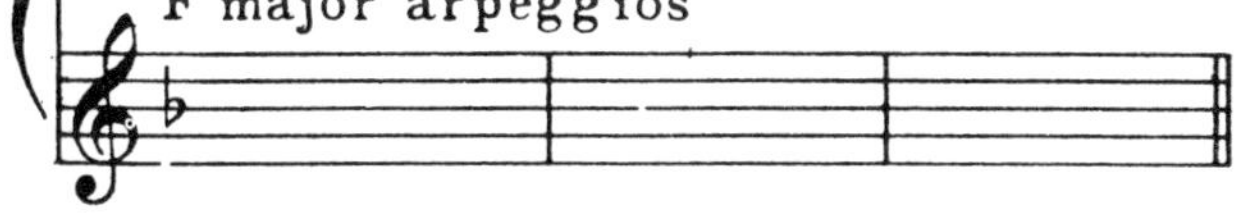

B♭ major chord positions

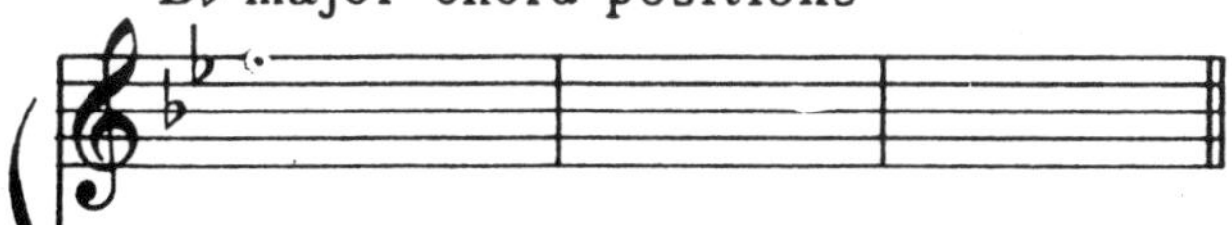

B♭ major arpeggios

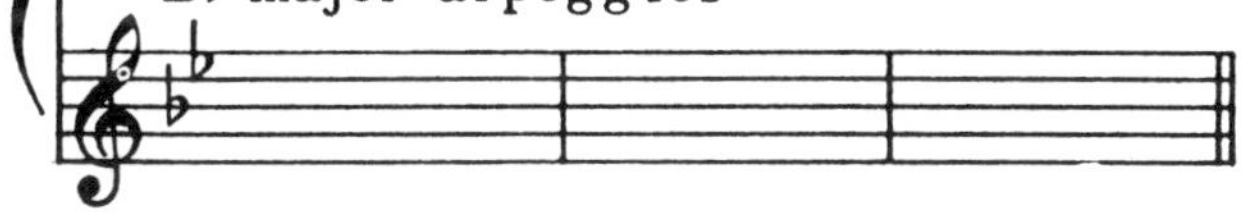

E♭ major chord positions

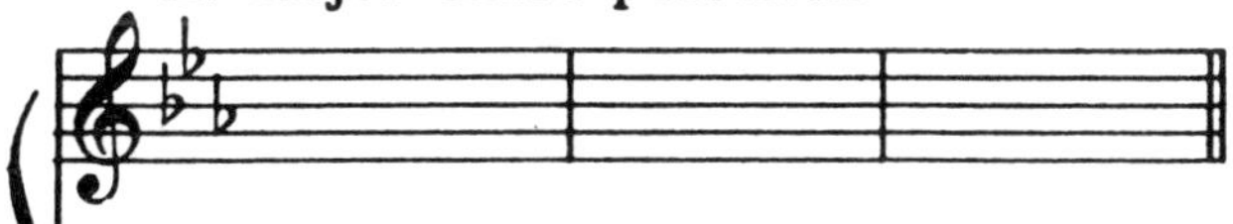

E♭ major arpeggios

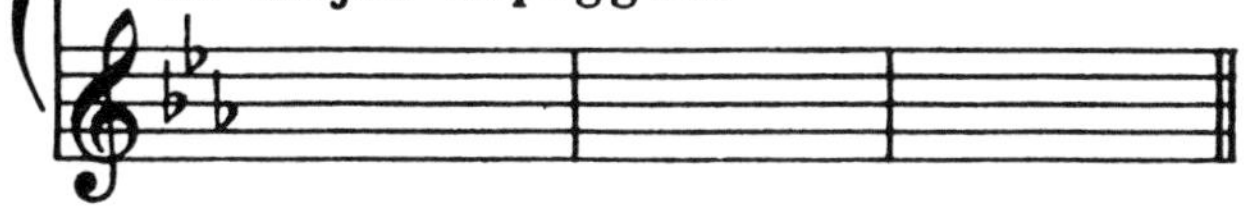

A♭ major chord positions

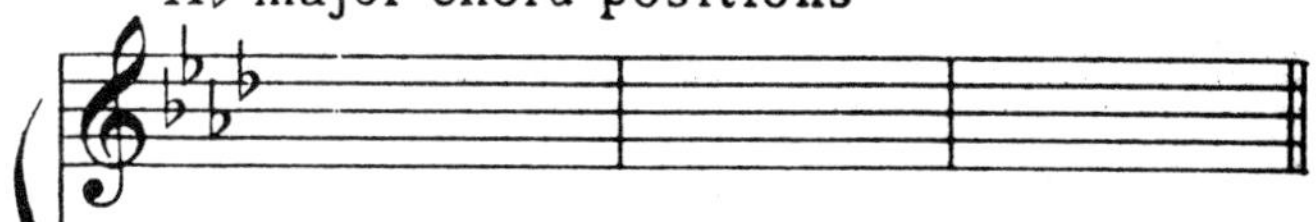

A♭ major arpeggios

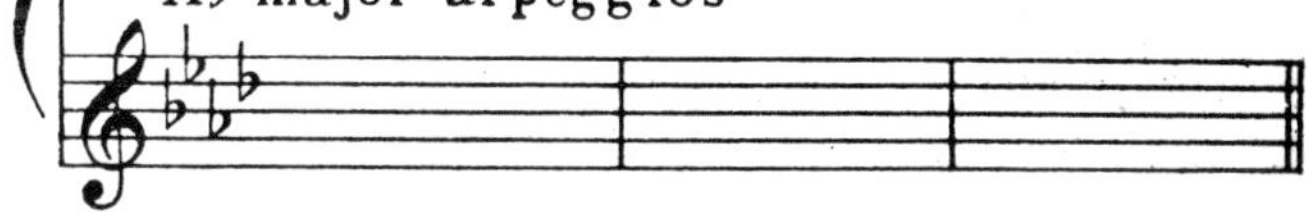

D♭ major chord positions

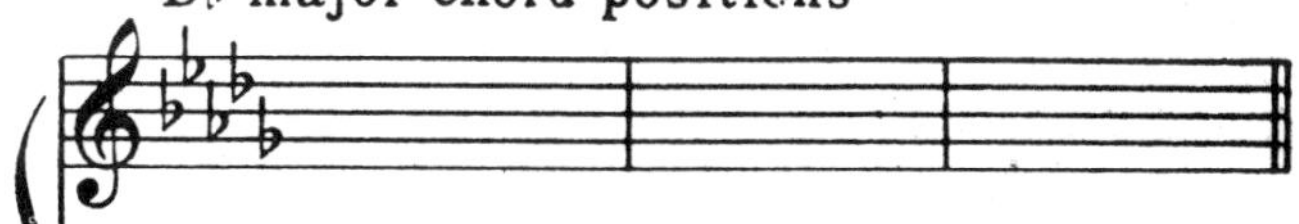

D♭ major arpeggios

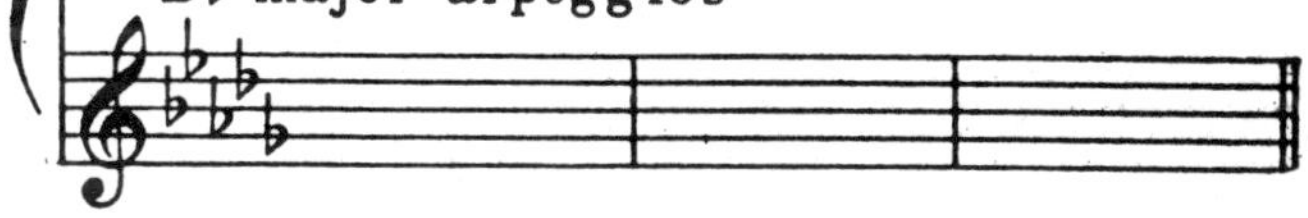

G♭ major chord positions

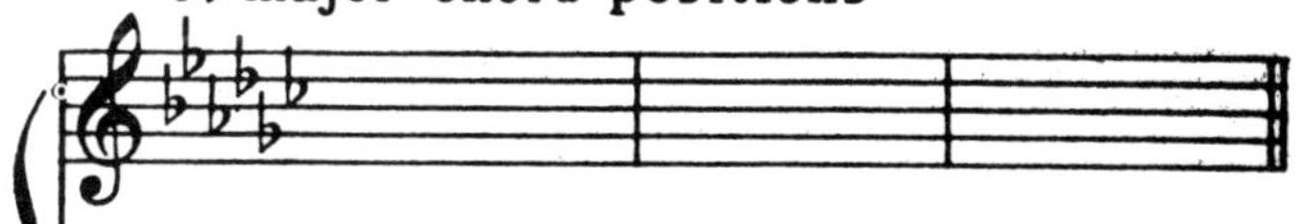

G♭ major arpeggios

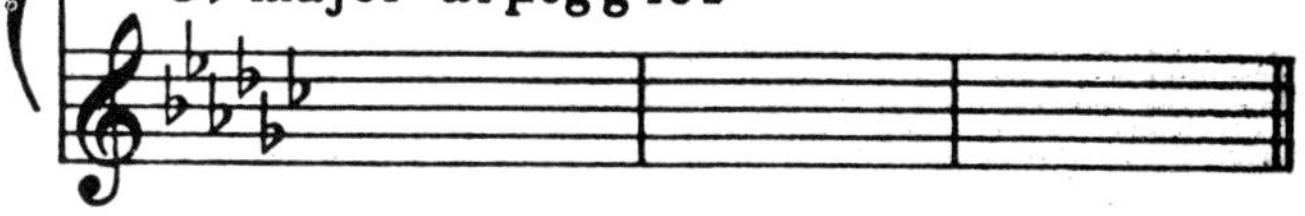

hands sep. 1st

F MAJOR ARPEGGIO

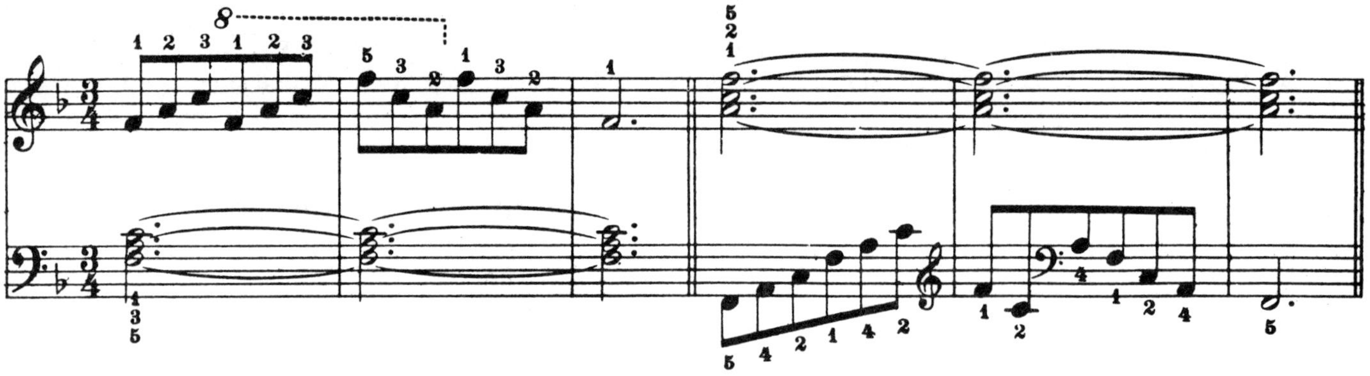

YANKEE DOODLE DANDY

Con brio

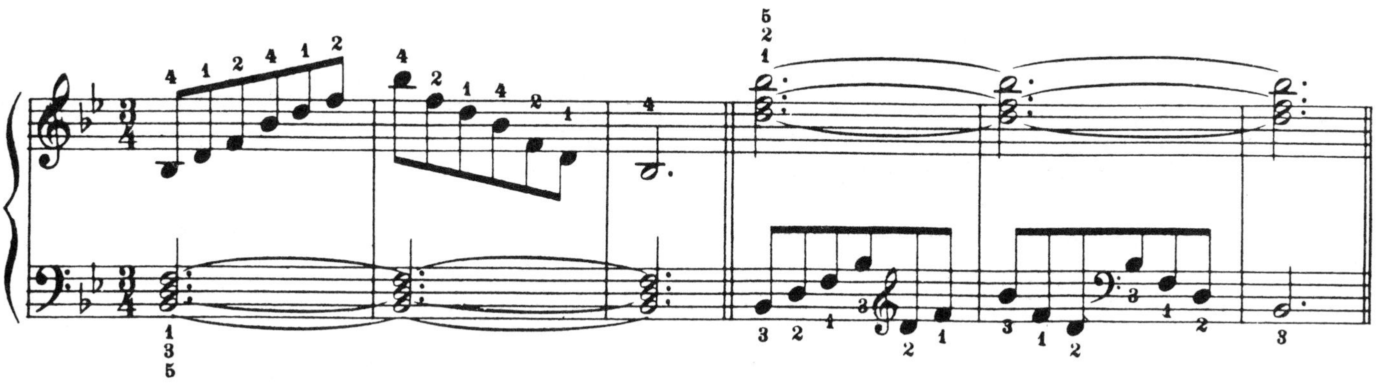

NOCTURNE

Hunten, Op. 181

E♭ MAJOR ARPEGGIO

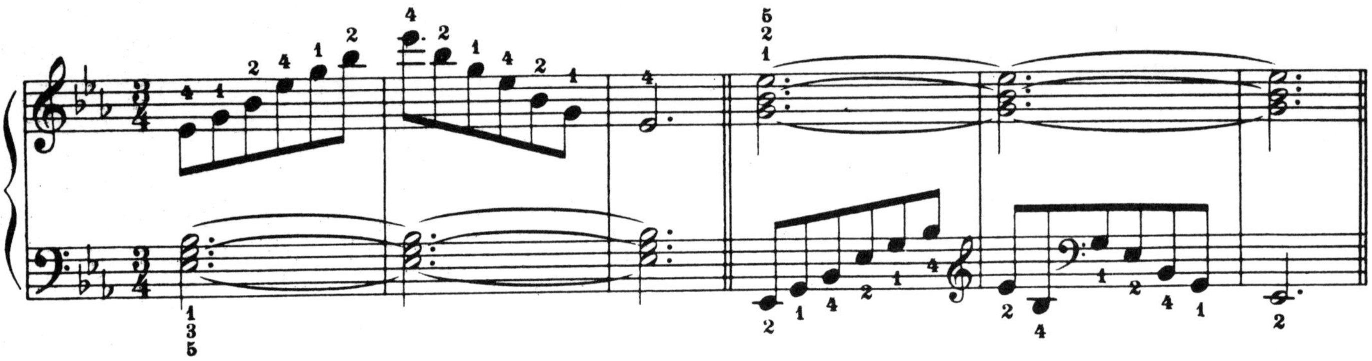

ANNIE LAURIE

William Douglas

Lady John Scott

Moderato

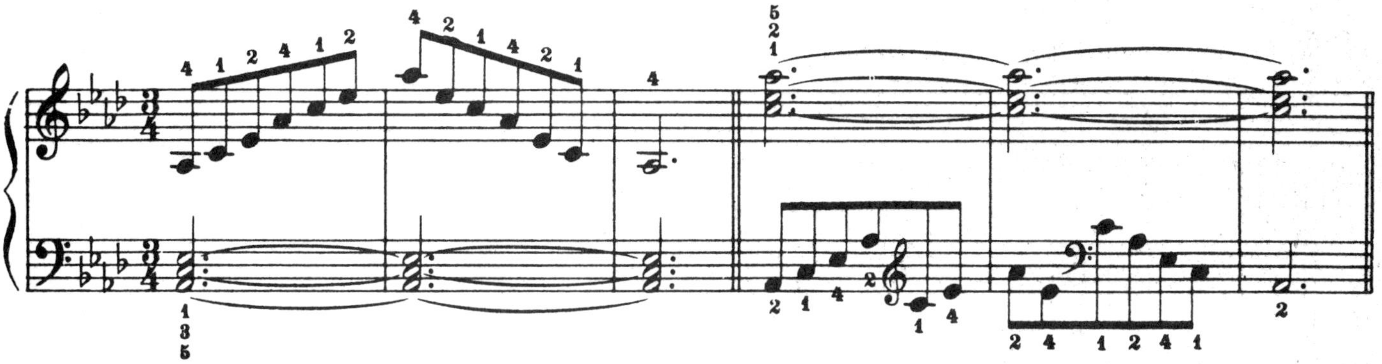

SPRING SHOWERS

Allegro

W. Fink

D♭ MAJOR ARPEGGIO

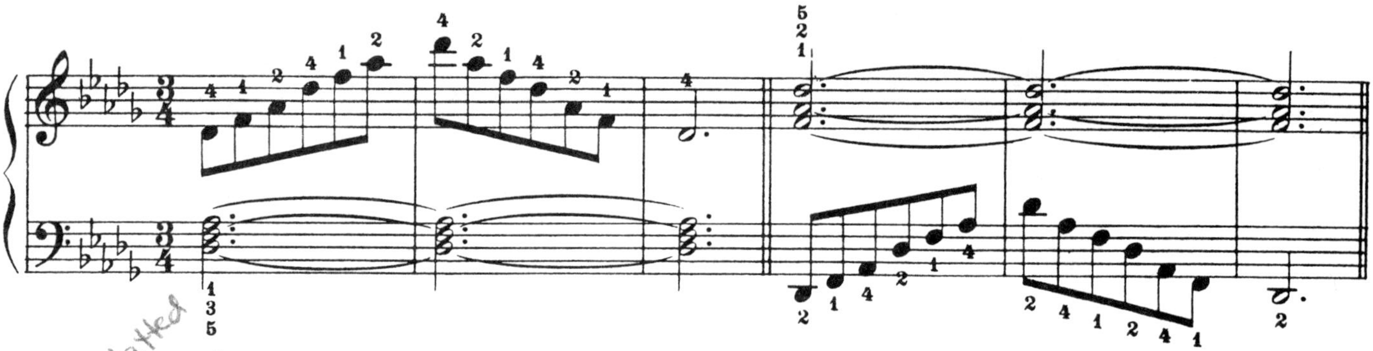

SANTA LUCIA

C + F not flatted
All black keys used

Andantino

Italian Folk Song

(B♭, E♭, A♭, D♭, G♭)

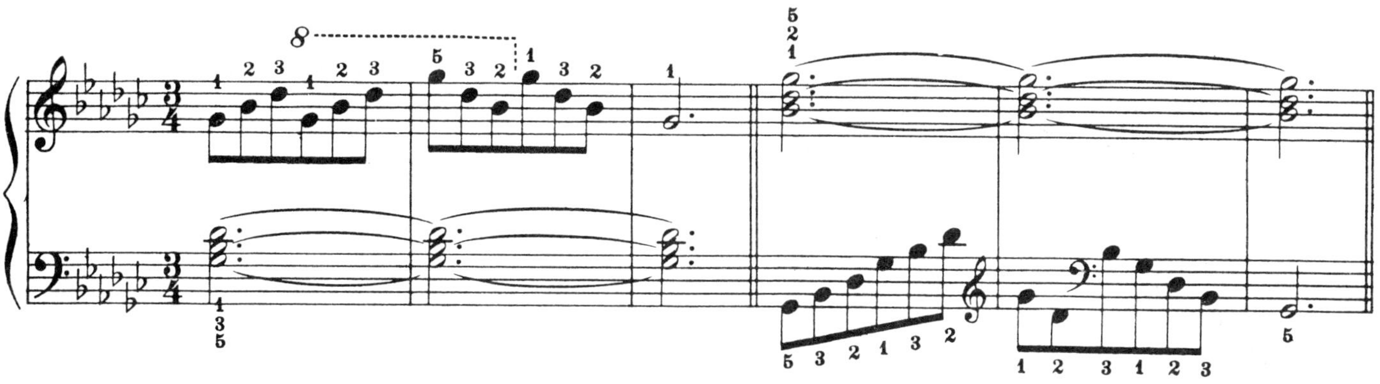

F not flatted

THE MANDOLIN SERENADE

Allegretto

E. Paladilhe

TONIC MINOR ARPEGGIOS IN SHARPS

Directions: Below are the principal minor sharp keys. You are to write in the three tonic chord positions and arpeggios for each key as you did before.

A minor chord positions

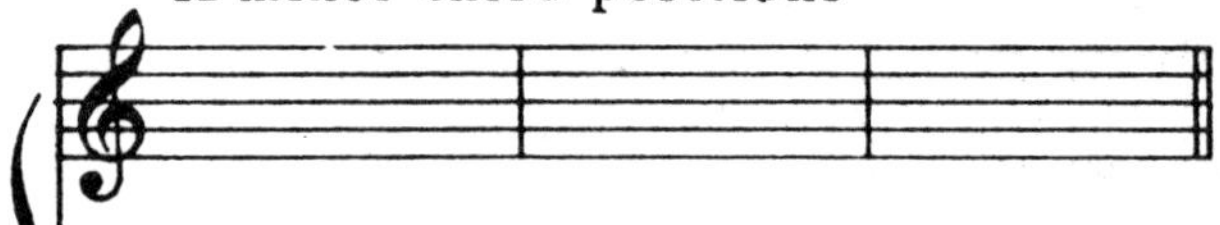

A minor arpeggios

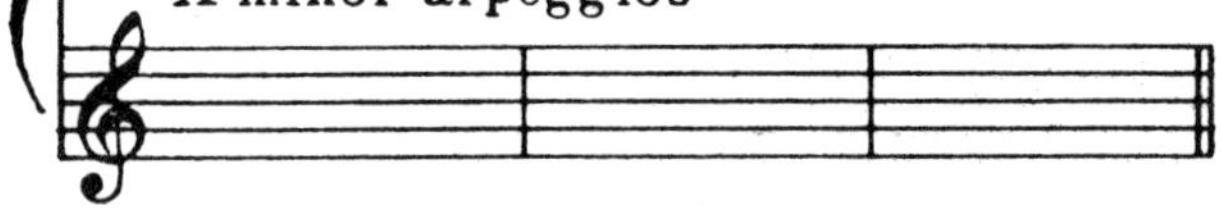

F♯ minor chord positions

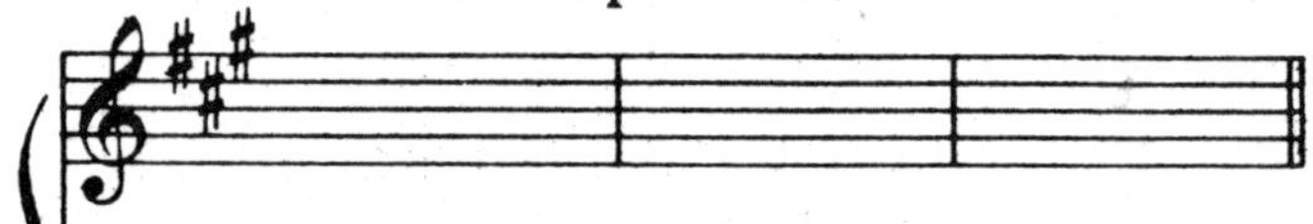

F♯ minor arpeggios

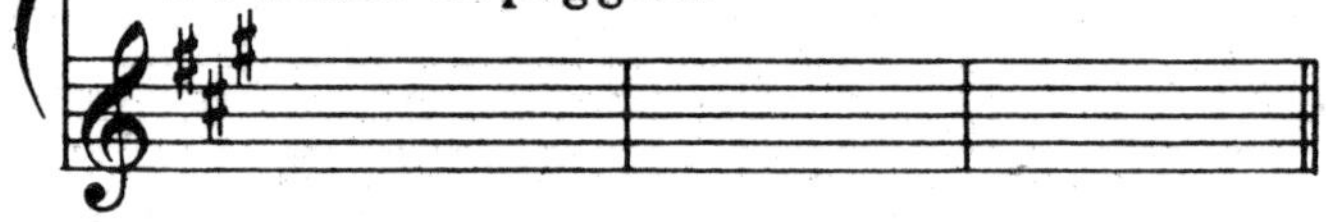

E minor chord positions

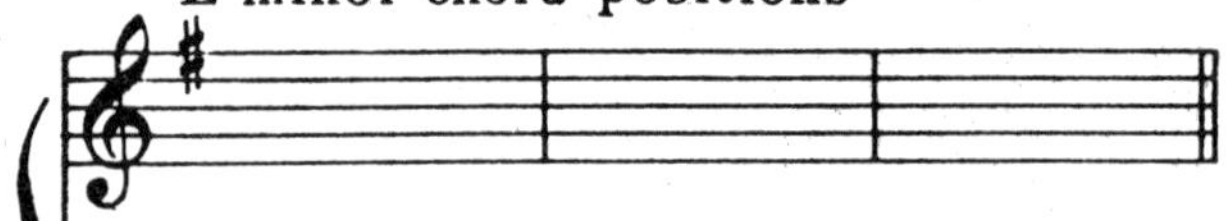

E minor arpeggios

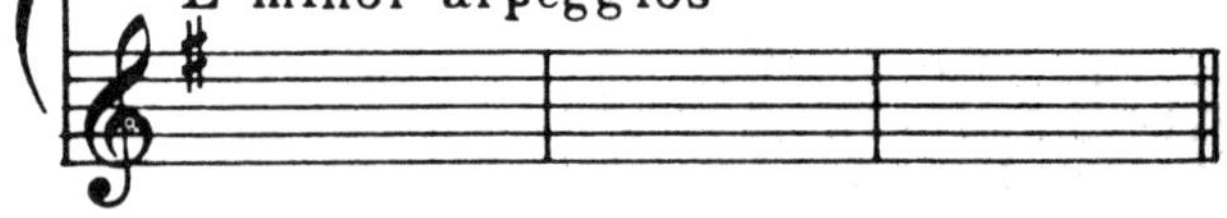

C♯ minor chord positions

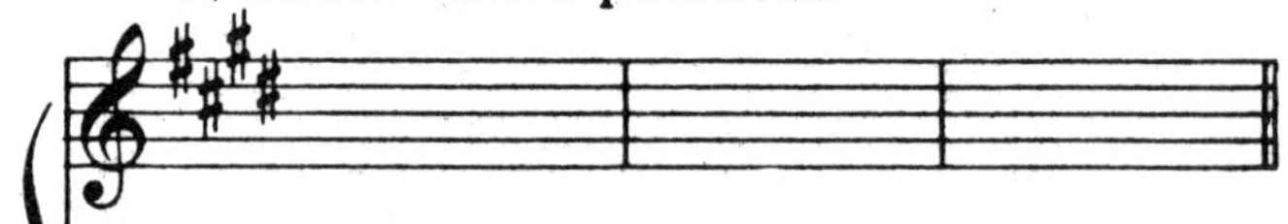

C♯ minor arpeggios

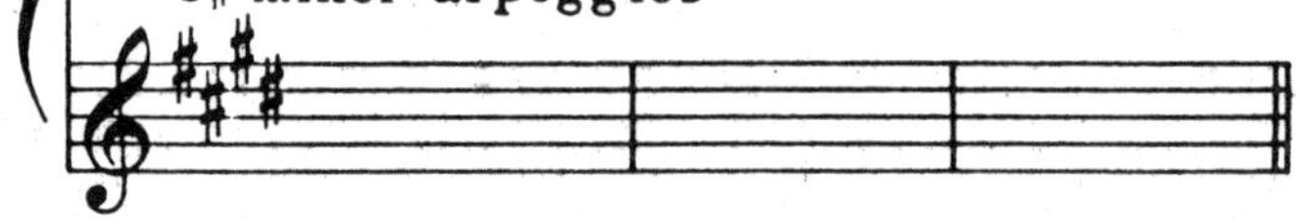

B minor chord positions

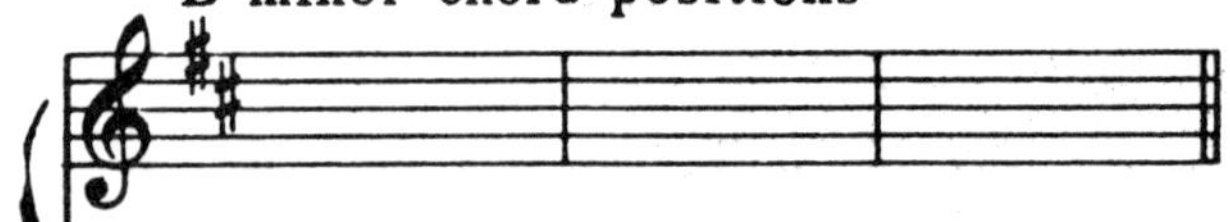

B minor arpeggios

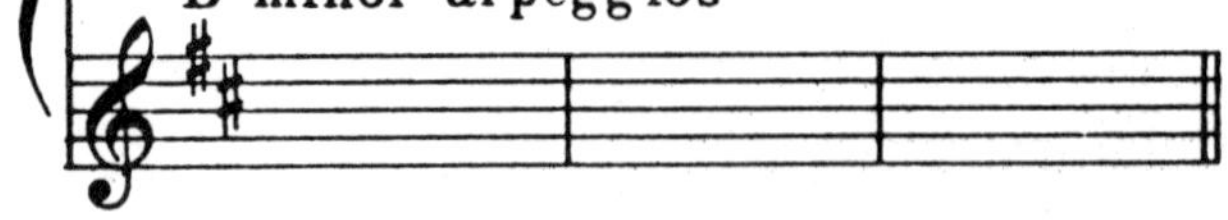

G♯ minor chord positions

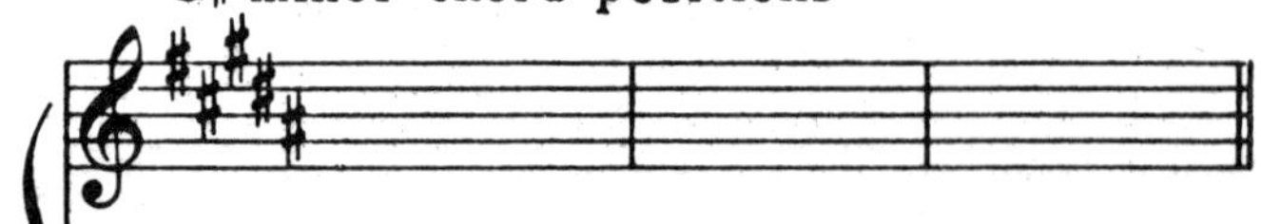

G♯ minor arpeggios

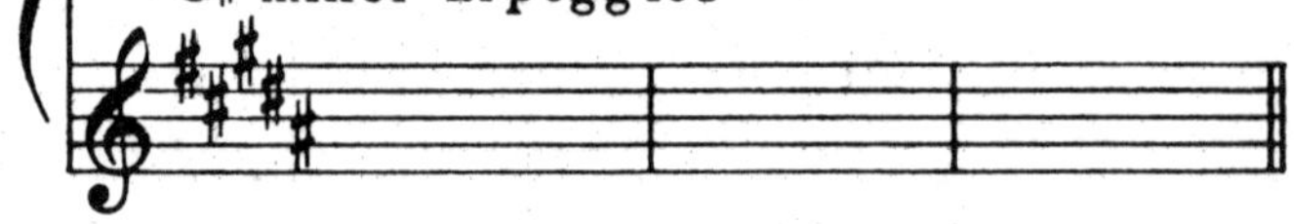

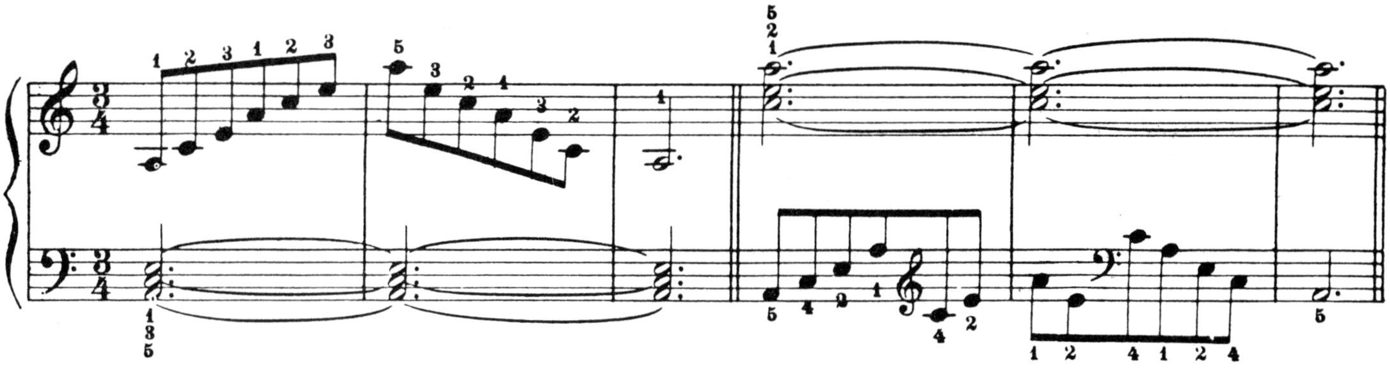

WALTZ

Allegretto

Brahms, Op.39, No.11

?. Do brackets mean only play together or hold?

E MINOR ARPEGGIO

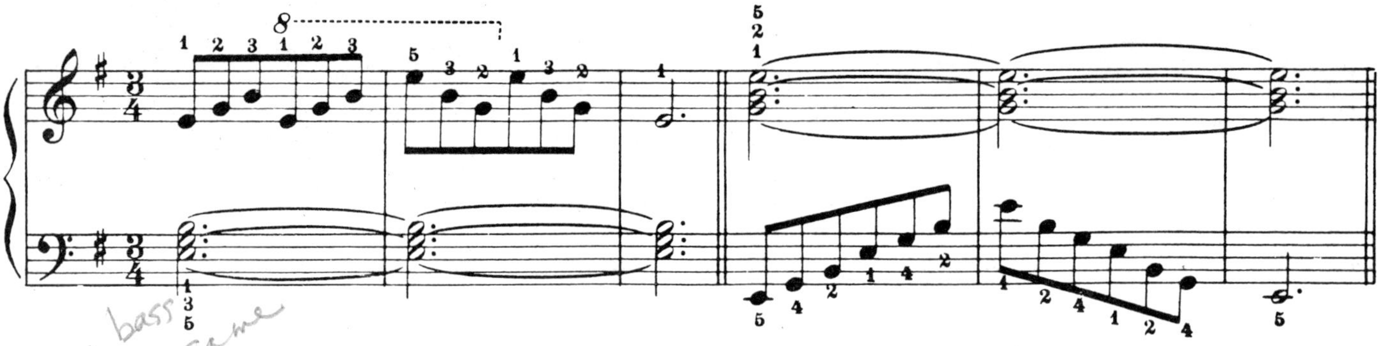

Note: every bass measure same

RUSSIAN DANCE

Presto

Tschaikowsky

B MINOR ARPEGGIO

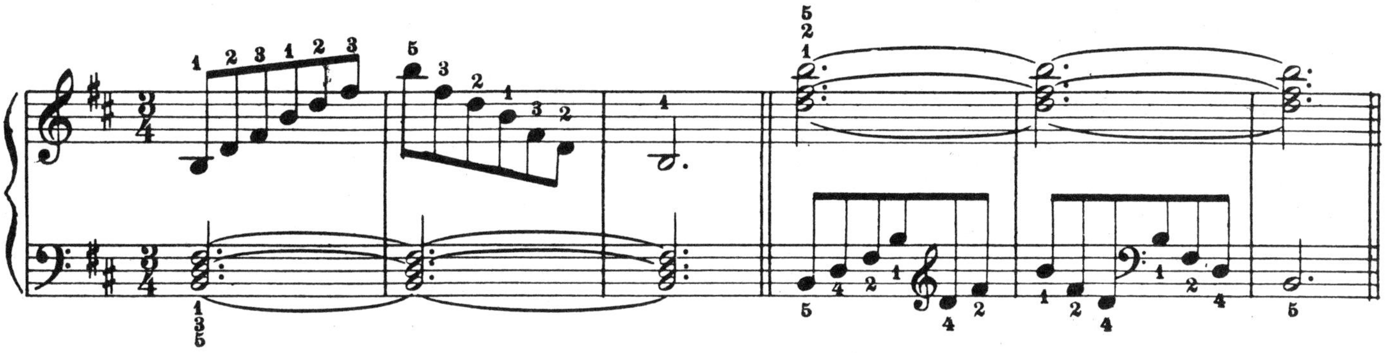

ELEGY

Adagio 1+2+3+4+

Jules Massenet

F♯ MINOR ARPEGGIO

JOHN ANDERSON MY JO

Moderato

Scottish Folk Song

C# MINOR ARPEGGIO

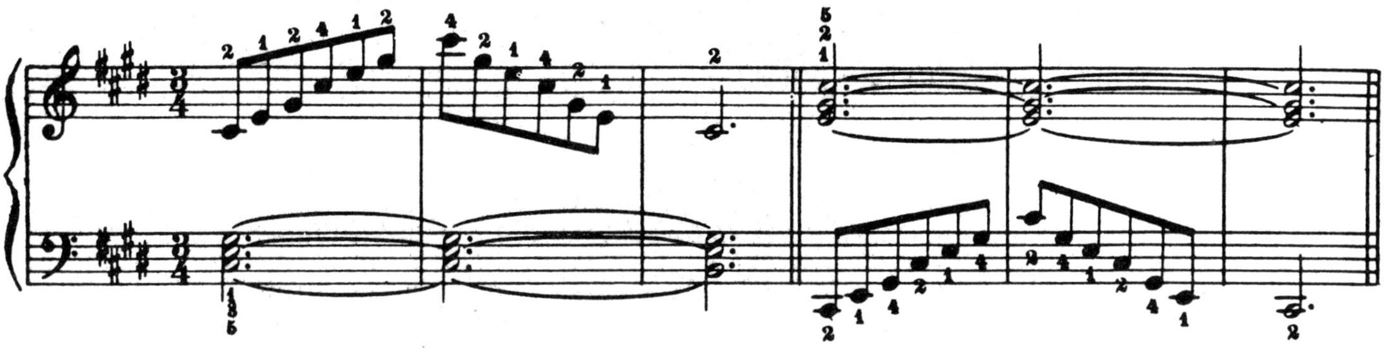

DARK EYES

Russian Folk Dance

Allegro

G♯ MINOR ARPEGGIO

PASSEPIED

Leo Delibes

TONIC MINOR ARPEGGIOS IN FLATS

Directions: Below are the principal minor flat keys. You are to write in the three tonic chord positions and arpeggios for each key as before.

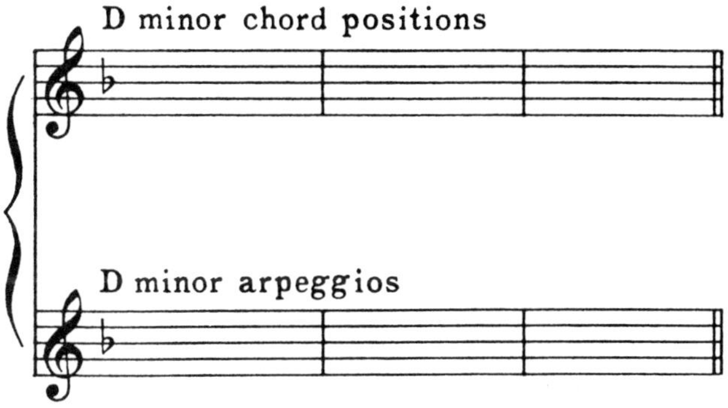

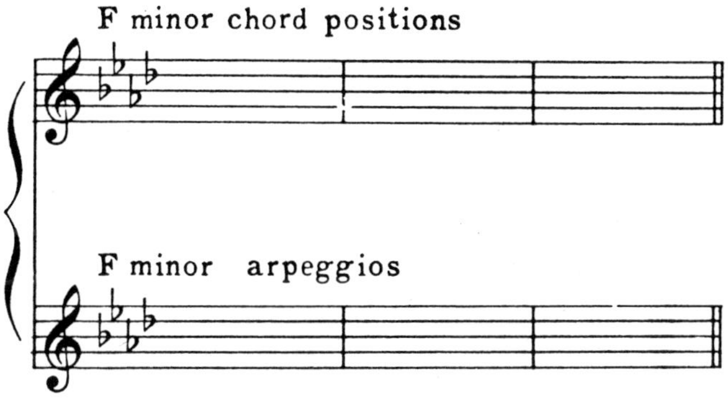

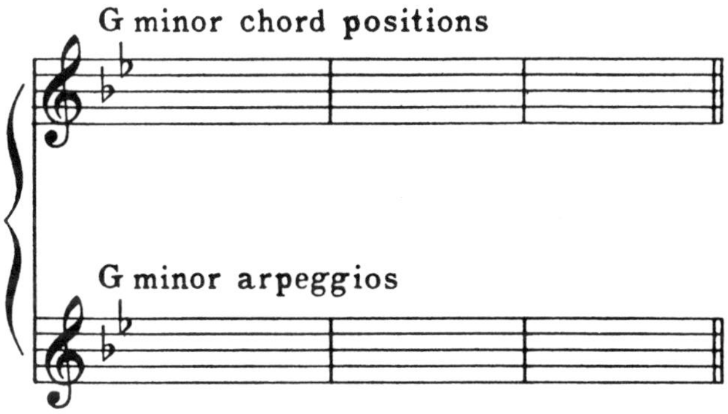

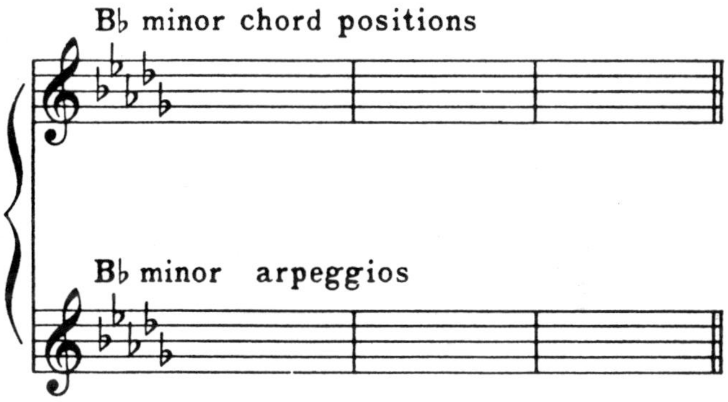

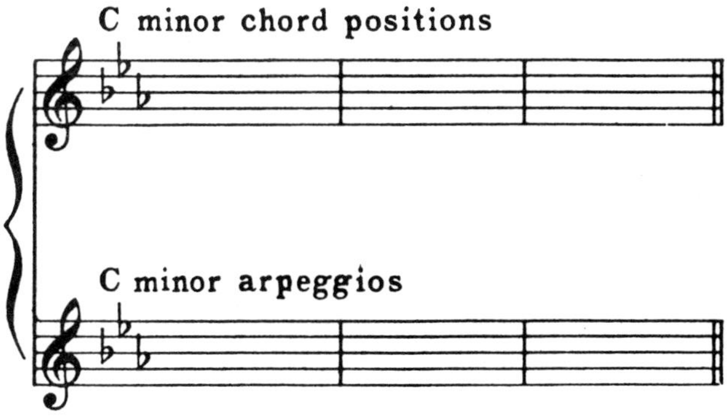

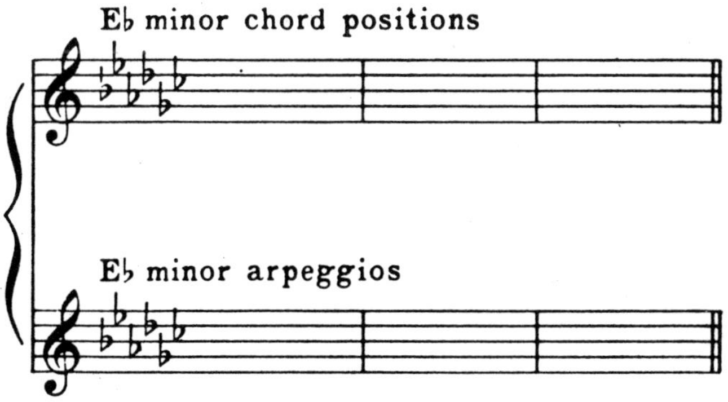

D MINOR ARPEGGIO

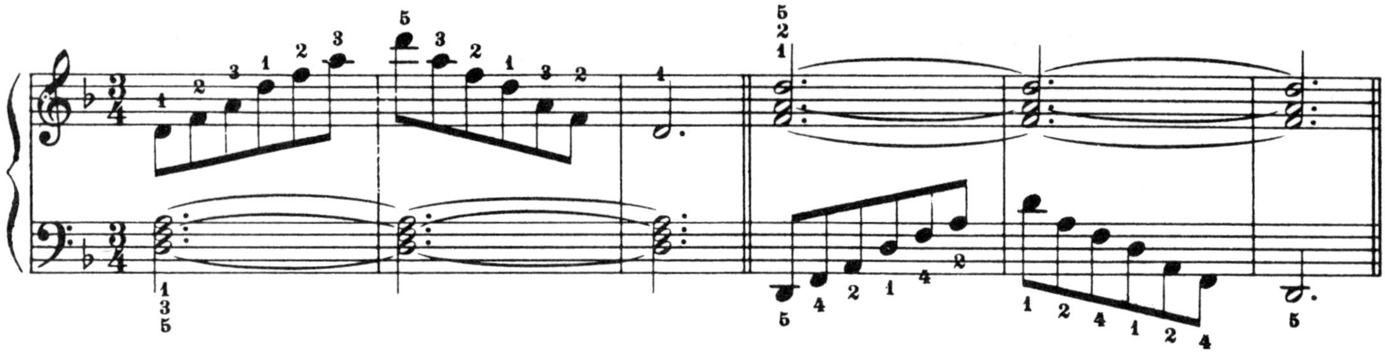

O CHARLIE IS MY DARLING

Moderato

Scotch Song

G MINOR ARPEGGIO

GO DOWN, MOSES

Plantation Spiritual

C MINOR ARPEGGIO

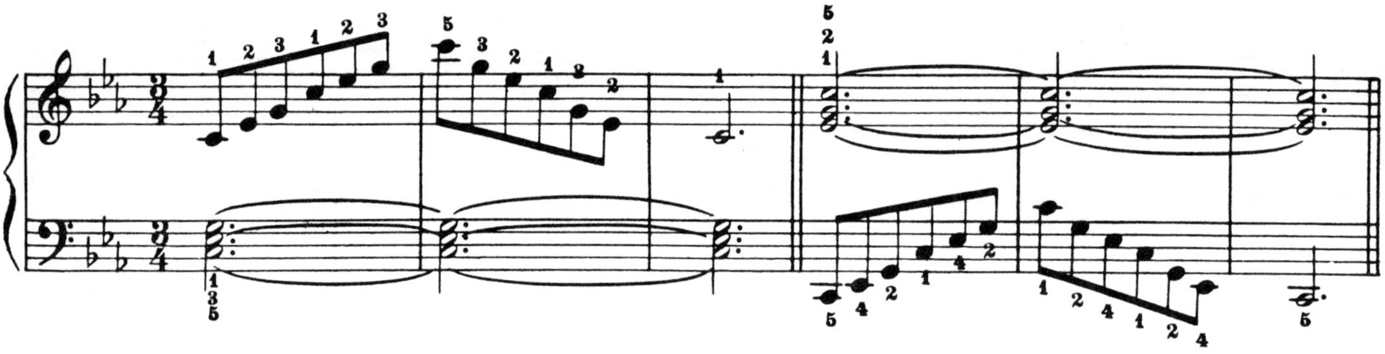

SONG OF THE VOLGA BOATMAN

Andante

Russian Folk Song

F MINOR ARPEGGIO

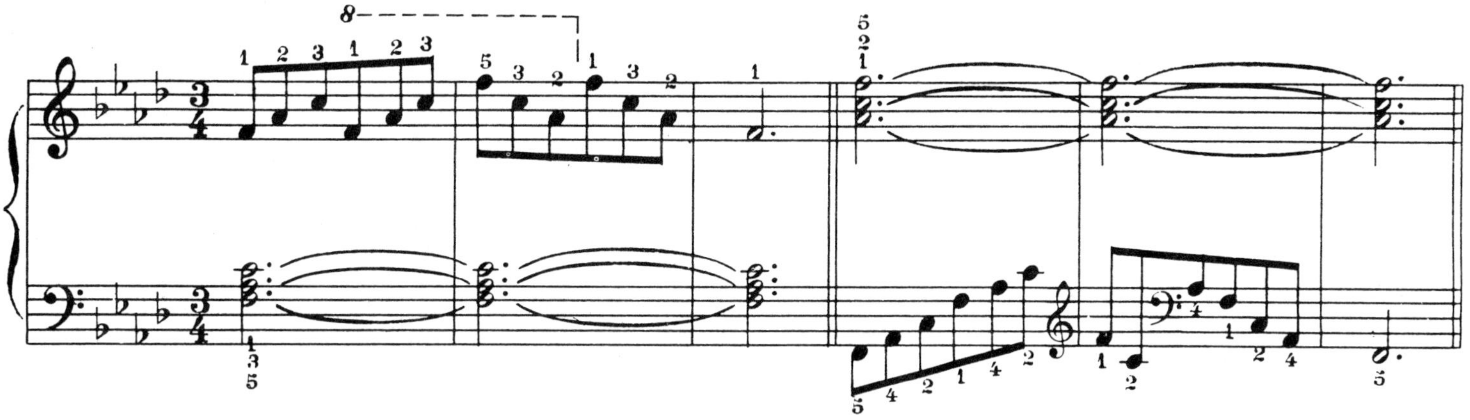

THE WRAGGLE-TAGGLE GYPSIES, O!

Moderato

Traditional

B♭ MINOR ARPEGGIO

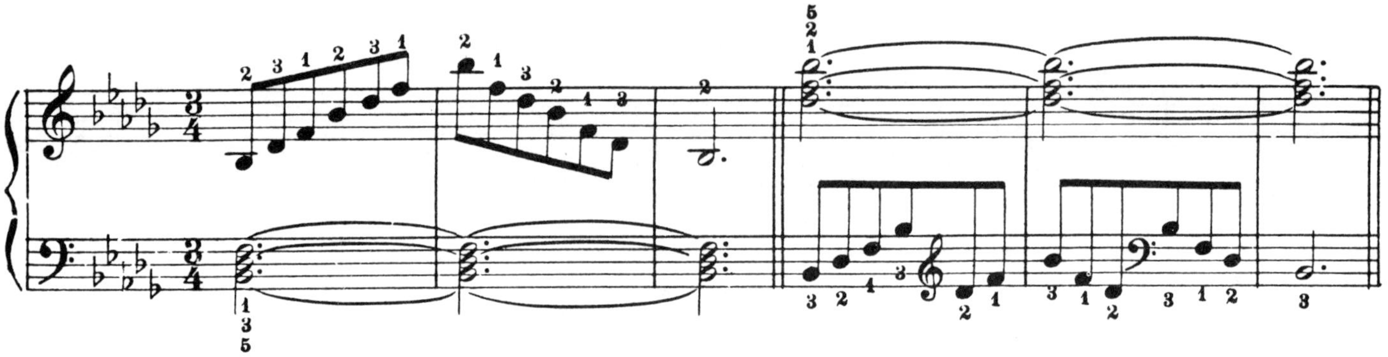

DARK WATERS

Le Carpentier, Op. 59, No. 12

MARCH SLAV

Tschaikowsky

Lento